I GOT 99 PROBLEMS...
BUT A PITCH AIN'T ONE

BUSINESS INSIGHTS FOR THE MEME AGE

BY COSTAS PAPAIKONOMOU

Copyright ©2021 Costas Papaikonomou

All rights reserved. No part of this book may be reproduced in any form or by any electronic or mechanical means including information storage and retrieval systems, without permission in writing from the author.

This is the first edition, April 2021

Twitter: @grumpyinnovator
Email: costas@grumpyinnovator.com
Web: grumpyinnovator.com

ISBN 9798739598721

**I GOT 99 PROBLEMS...
BUT A PITCH AIN'T ONE**

*to all my fellow design & innovation team
colleagues over the past 25 years.*

*And a massive thanks to IMGFLP whose online tool
I used for all these memes, visit them to make yours.*

COPY SUCCESSFUL CEO LIFE HACKS

LIKELY OUTCOMES

Putting six juniors together and calling it an incubator isn't innovation

I GOT 99 PROBLEMS...
BUT A PITCH AIN'T ONE

EVER

SIX SIGMA TEAM
OPTIMIZING FACTORY
PERFORMANCE

GUY WITH SPANNER
WHO ACTUALLY KNOWS
HOW THE LINE WORKS

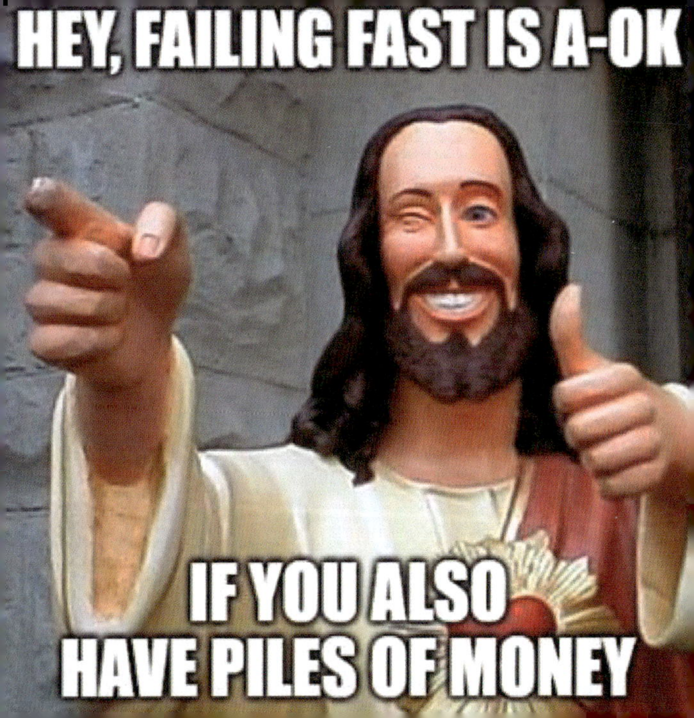
HEY, FAILING FAST IS A-OK
IF YOU ALSO
HAVE PILES OF MONEY

**I GOT 99 PROBLEMS...
BUT A PITCH AIN'T ONE**

I THOUGHT WE WERE A TEAM

THERE IS NO "I" IN "BLAME"

Weekdays	Weekends
Analyzing decision tree data like a g'damn hero	Stock up on BOGOF

KNOWS ALL ACRONYMS

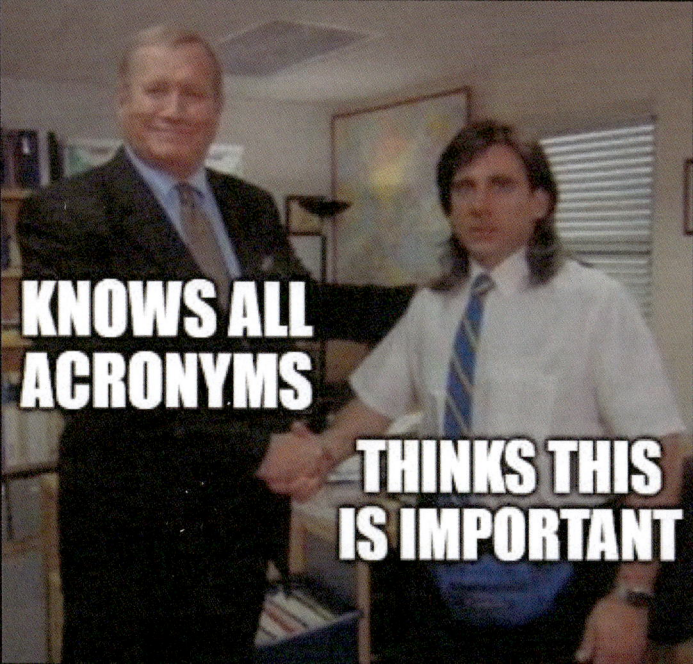

THINKS THIS IS IMPORTANT

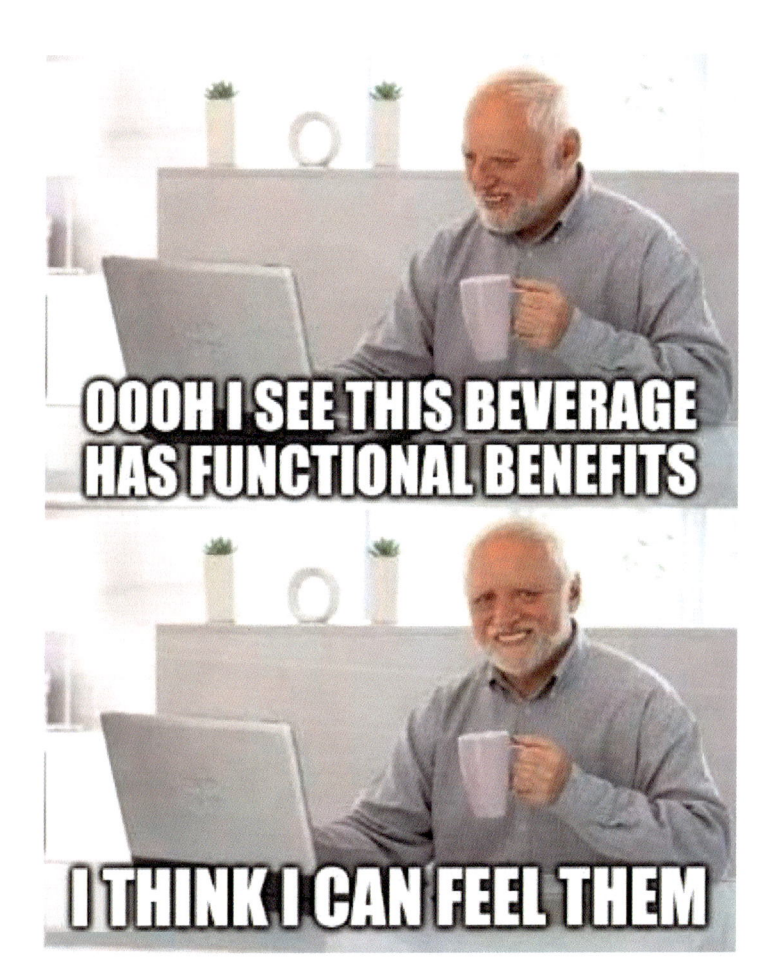

OOOH I SEE THIS BEVERAGE HAS FUNCTIONAL BENEFITS

I THINK I CAN FEEL THEM

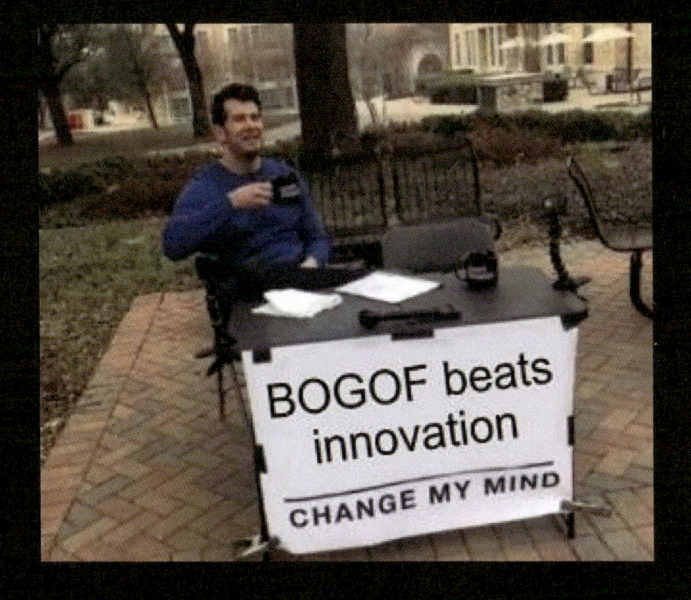

**I GOT 99 PROBLEMS...
BUT A PITCH AIN'T ONE**

BOGOF beats innovation

CHANGE MY MIND

MY PRODUCT ON SHELF

MY PRODUCT WITH BOGOF

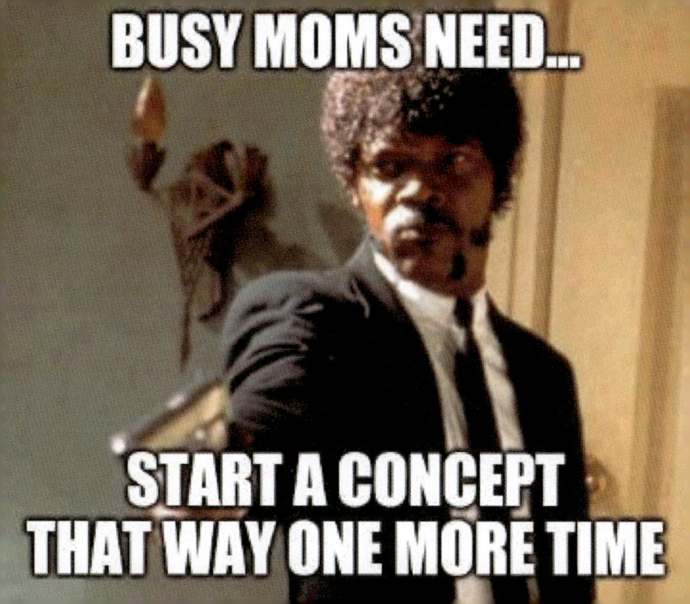
BUSY MOMS NEED...
START A CONCEPT
THAT WAY ONE MORE TIME

I BLEW MY BUDGET ON VALIDATING IDEAS

I COULD HAVE BRIBED STAKEHOLDERS FOR LESS

I GOT 99 PROBLEMS...
BUT A PITCH AIN'T ONE

WHEN YOU REALIZE THE REAL WORLD DOESN'T FOLLOW BUSINESS BOOK RULES

(confused unga bunga)

WHAT DO YOU THINK OF MY MARKET VOLUME ESTIMATES? STRONG CASE, EH?

DISTRIBUTION IS NEVER 100% AT LAUNCH, NOR IS AWARENESS AND THEY NEVER WILL BE.

**I GOT 99 PROBLEMS...
BUT A PITCH AIN'T ONE**

COMPETITOR FAILURE

when you cherry-picked consumers for your concept test

But no one needs to as you'll be long gone by the time they launch

BRAND MANAGER
BRAND EXTENSION INTO ADJACENT TERRITORY
CURRENT BRAND LOVERS
OUT OF SCOPE FOREVER

BENEFIT HIERARCHY

	Works Better
	Chocolate Covered
	3D Printed
	Cloud Connected

I GOT 99 PROBLEMS...
BUT A PITCH AIN'T ONE

HEEERE'S THE CURRENT MARKET LEADER

AFTER YOU THOUGHT THEY WOULDN'T RESPOND TO YOUR CHALLENGER LAUNCH

OPPORTUNITY DIG SITES

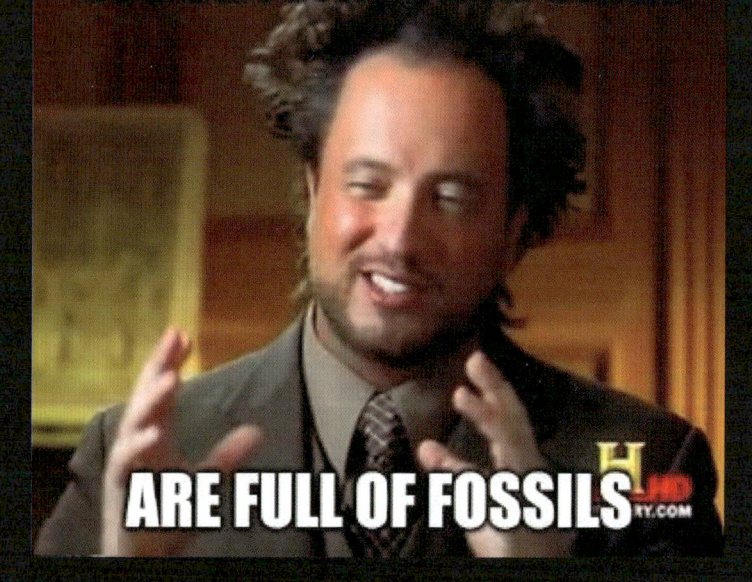

ARE FULL OF FOSSILS

**I GOT 99 PROBLEMS...
BUT A PITCH AIN'T ONE**

NEW BRAND MANAGER

HOT COMPETITOR LAUNCH

R&D AND OPS WHO JUST SPENT TWO YEARS DEVELOPING HIS PREDECESSOR'S PRODUCT

SHOW ME ON THIS DOLL WHICH PART NOW NEEDS MORE GOOD BACTERIA

I GOT 99 PROBLEMS...
BUT A PITCH AIN'T ONE

US OLD FOLKS REALLY JUST WANT EASY-OPEN PACKAGING.

NOOOOOO YOU WANT VITALITY BENEFITS THRU NOSTALGIC RECIPEEEEEES

EBITDAAAAAAAA

WE WILL FIGHT A BIT SHADY

I GOT 99 PROBLEMS...
BUT A PITCH AIN'T ONE

LEFT
EXIT 12

Happiness & Peace of Mind

Divorce & Financial Ruin

Take a breakthrough product idea to market

OBPCC   5P

EBIDTA

SUPPLY CHAIN, R&D AND DISTRIBUTION RESTRUCTURING
CEO'S GREEN PLEDGE

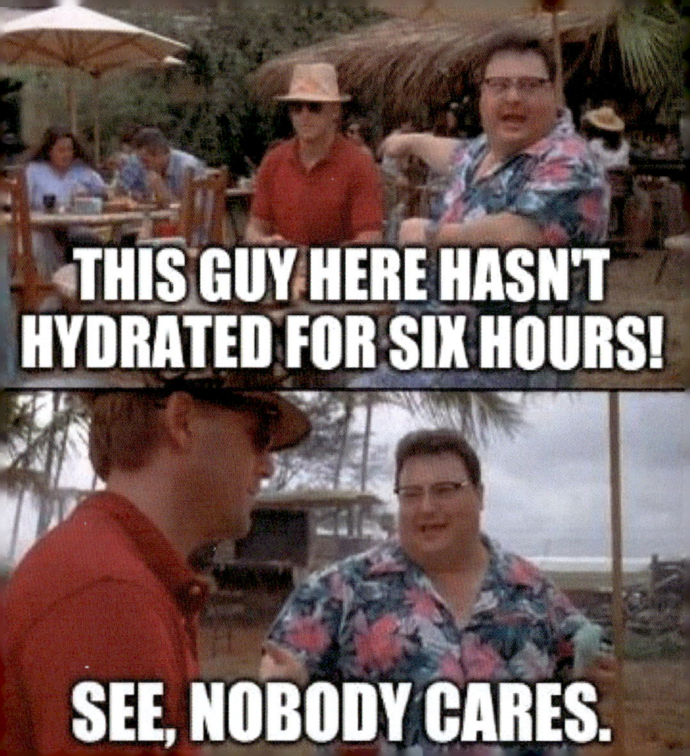
THIS GUY HERE HASN'T HYDRATED FOR SIX HOURS!
SEE, NOBODY CARES.

WELCOME TO HORIZON 3
YOU ARE SAFE NOW.
REALITY DOESN'T COUNT HERE.

PUTTING THE NO BACK IN IN-NO-VATION

I GOT 99 PROBLEMS...
BUT A PITCH AIN'T ONE

INVINCIBLE

Sugar

Polyethylene

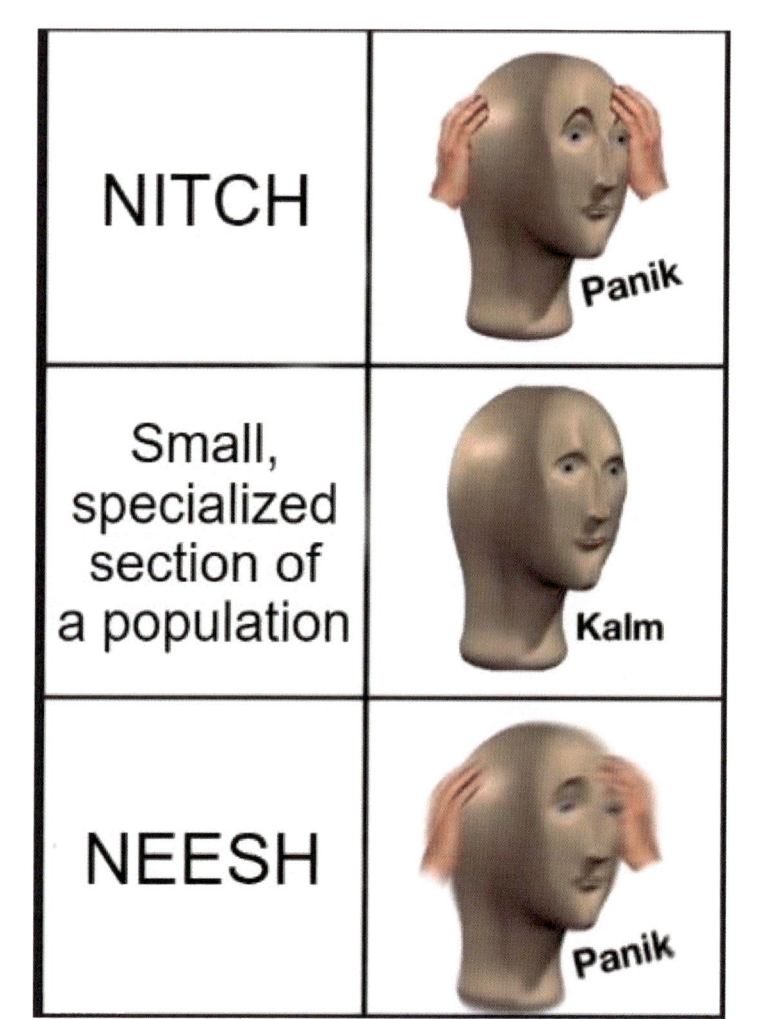

NITCH	Panik
Small, specialized section of a population	Kalm
NEESH	Panik

Did you upload the system virus to trigger full meltdown!?
It's not an IoT connected fridge, I just left the freezer door open

YOUR CONCEPT SCORED 'RISKY' BUT UR LAUNCHING ANYWAY

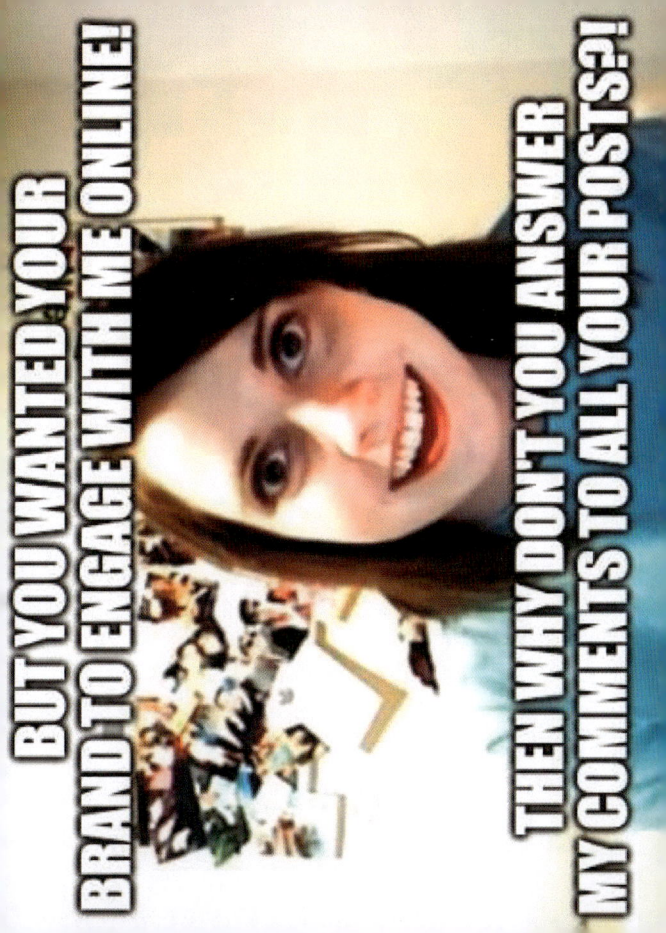

BUT YOU WANTED YOUR BRAND TO ENGAGE WITH ME ONLINE!

THEN WHY DON'T YOU ANSWER MY COMMENTS TO ALL YOUR POSTS?!

Hard to swallow pills

MAINSTREAM CONSUMERS

DON'T CHANGE BEHAVIOUR TO BE GREENER

THEY EXPECT MANUFACTURERS TO DO IT FOR THEM

I GOT 99 PROBLEMS...
BUT A PITCH AIN'T ONE

WHAT IF I TOLD YOU

WE ARE ALL JUST A PERSONA IN SOMEONE'S SEGMENTATION STUDY

Pentagon

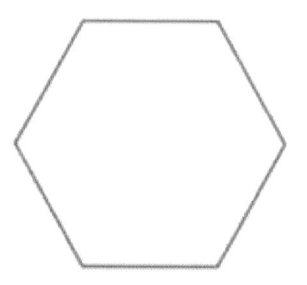

Hexagon

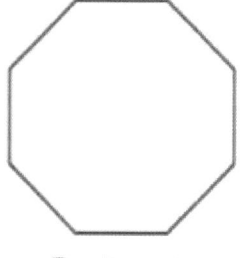

Octagon

Margin gone

I GOT 99 PROBLEMS...
BUT A PITCH AIN'T ONE

YOUR MODELS PROVE THIS WILL WORK, RIGHT?

YES

OBPPC

OPERATIONAL EXCELLENCE TEAM

BREAKTHROUGH PRODUCT LAUNCH

You can get paid to answer surveys about products you never bought nor consumed.

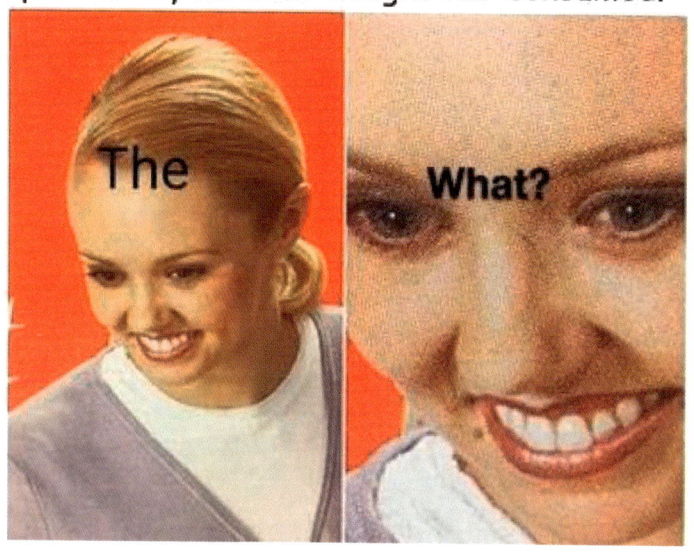

The What?

I GOT 99 PROBLEMS...
BUT A PITCH AIN'T ONE

Some PC ambition by 2025 | Pledge

I MADE A GREEN PLEDGE FOR 2025

NOW YOU GO MAKE IT SEEM LIKE WE'RE ON TRACK

**I GOT 99 PROBLEMS...
BUT A PITCH AIN'T ONE**

YOU CAN'T FAIL THE CONCEPT SCREENER

IF YOU WRITE YOUR OWN QUESTIONNAIRE

INNOVATE IN THE
WHITE SPACES THEY SAID
AND THEY SAY
I AM THE RACIST

IF YOU RE-LAUNCH THE PRODUCT YOU DE-LISTED BEFORE

DOES THAT COUNT AS INNOVATION?

YOU SAID THIS PACK MATERIAL WAS SUSTAINABLE!
IT'S RECYCLABLE FFS!
Orange County
NOT IF THERE'S NO RECYCLING INFRASTRUCTURE!
THAT'S JUST LANDFILL, MORON!
MAKE IT DEGRADABLE OR WE'RE GOING BACK TO EDIBLE PACKAGING YOU HEAR ME?!

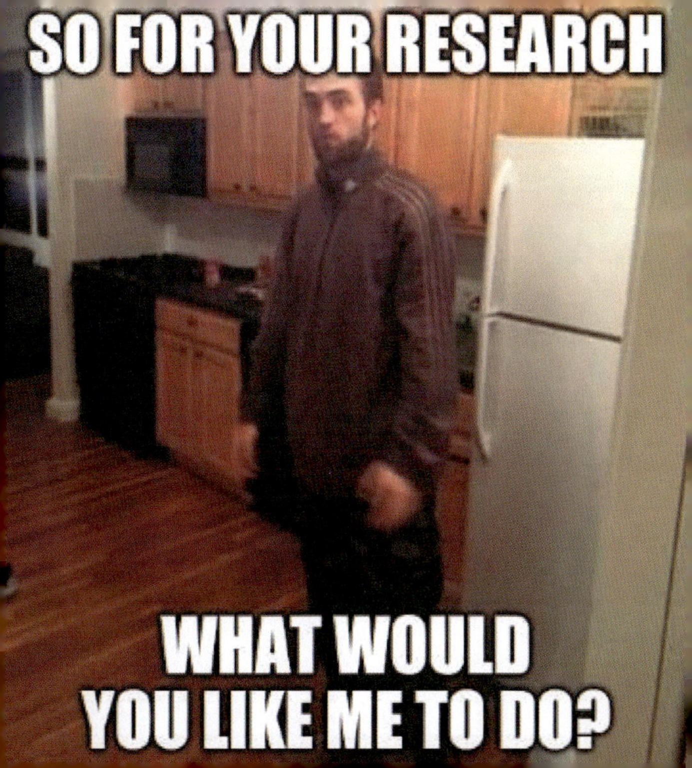
SO FOR YOUR RESEARCH
WHAT WOULD
YOU LIKE ME TO DO?

BRAND MARKETING BOSS

REALIZING THE CORE BENEFIT WAS MADE UP BY A PREDECESSOR

I GOT 99 PROBLEMS...
BUT A PITCH AIN'T ONE

THERE ARE NO STUPID IDEAS

ONLY STUPID PEOPLE

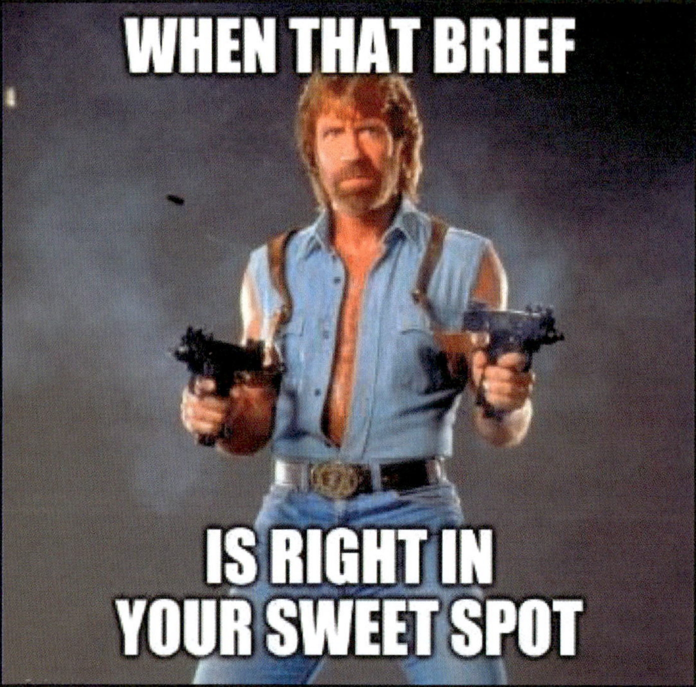
WHEN THAT BRIEF
IS RIGHT IN
YOUR SWEET SPOT

I GOT 99 PROBLEMS...
BUT A PITCH AIN'T ONE

MY PRODUCT IDEA KEEPS FAILING TO PASS VALIDATION

SAY IT'S COVERED IN CHOCOLATE AND YOU CAN WIN PRIZES

🙅	Run test launch in small pilot to get real market results.
👉	Run quant test at same price of which you can manipulate data.

CONSUMERS LOVE TRADITIONAL REMEDIES

ESPECIALLY SINCE I FIRED MY R&D DEPT

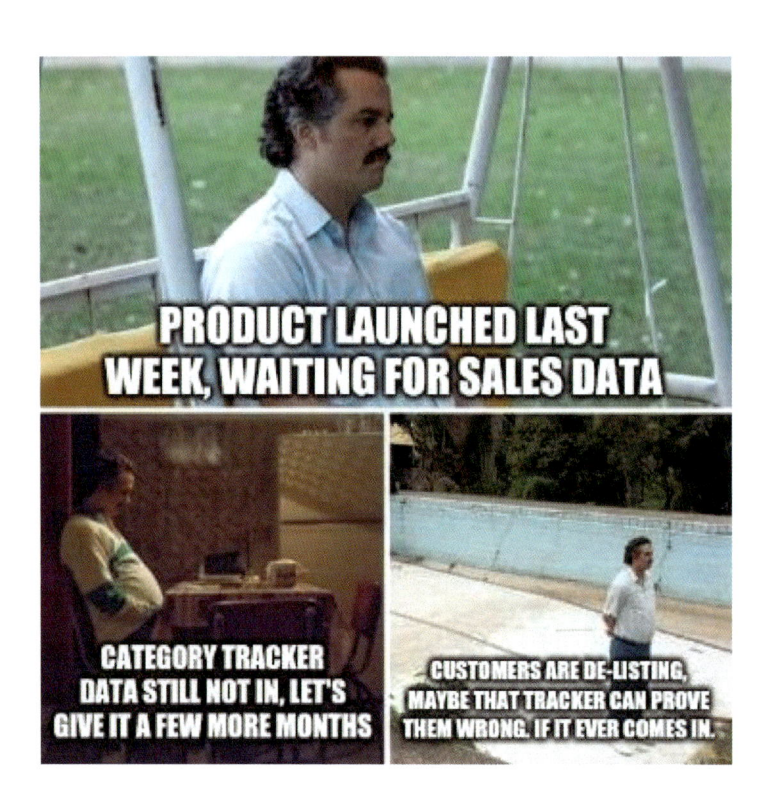

PRODUCT LAUNCHED LAST WEEK, WAITING FOR SALES DATA

CATEGORY TRACKER DATA STILL NOT IN, LET'S GIVE IT A FEW MORE MONTHS

CUSTOMERS ARE DE-LISTING, MAYBE THAT TRACKER CAN PROVE THEM WRONG. IF IT EVER COMES IN.

I GOT 99 PROBLEMS...
BUT A PITCH AIN'T ONE

SO ANY PRODUCT I EVER LAUNCH WILL ALWAYS HAVE TO DISPLACE AN EXISTING ONE?

YES SON. WHITE SPACES ARE A MYTH.

BUT WE CAN KEEP THAT OUR SECRET, AND JUST PRETEND OTHERWISE

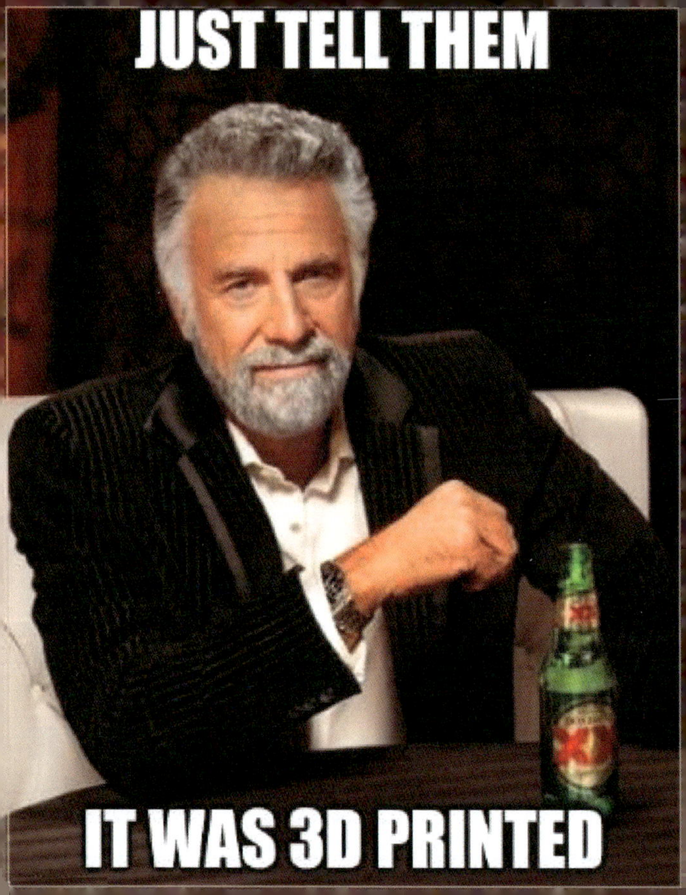
JUST TELL THEM
IT WAS 3D PRINTED

**I GOT 99 PROBLEMS...
BUT A PITCH AIN'T ONE**

FRANTIC PIVOTING BY HIGH BURNRATE STARTUPS

REAL ENTREPRENEURS WITH POSITIVE CASHFLOW

YOU MEAN FEASIBLE?
NO, AFFORDABLE.
CAPTAIN AMERICA
CIVIL WAR
MAY 6, 2016

**I GOT 99 PROBLEMS...
BUT A PITCH AIN'T ONE**

WHEN A PERSON YOU HIRED STRAIGHT OUT OF UNI RESIGNS TO JOIN OTHER COMPANY

YOU WERE THE CHOSEN ONE

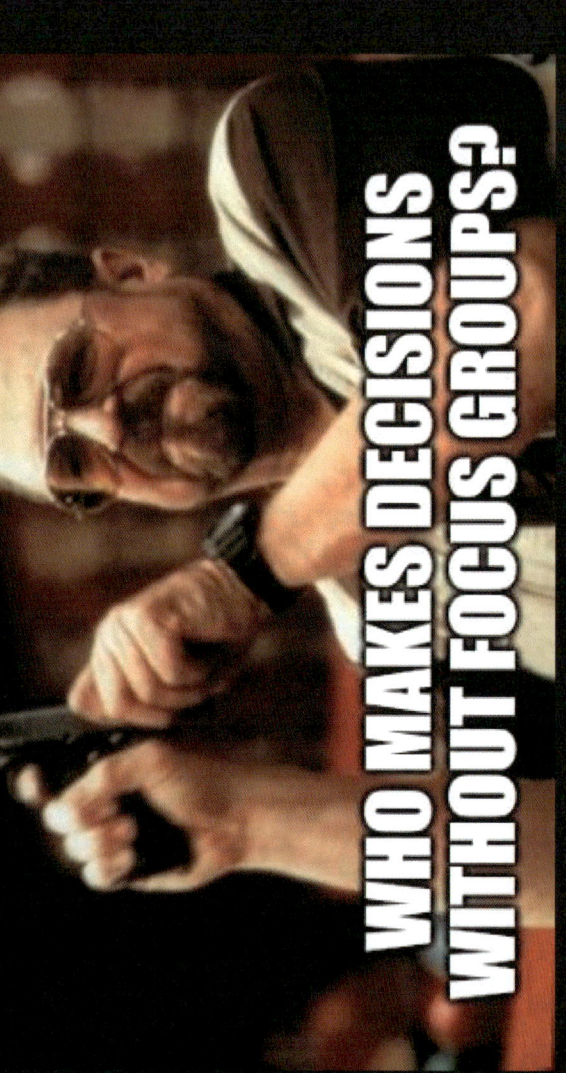

AM I THE ONLY ONE AROUND HERE WHO MAKES DECISIONS WITHOUT FOCUS GROUPS?

I GOT 99 PROBLEMS...
BUT A PITCH AIN'T ONE

Never had.

Wait, 'purchase intent' has no actual predictive value?

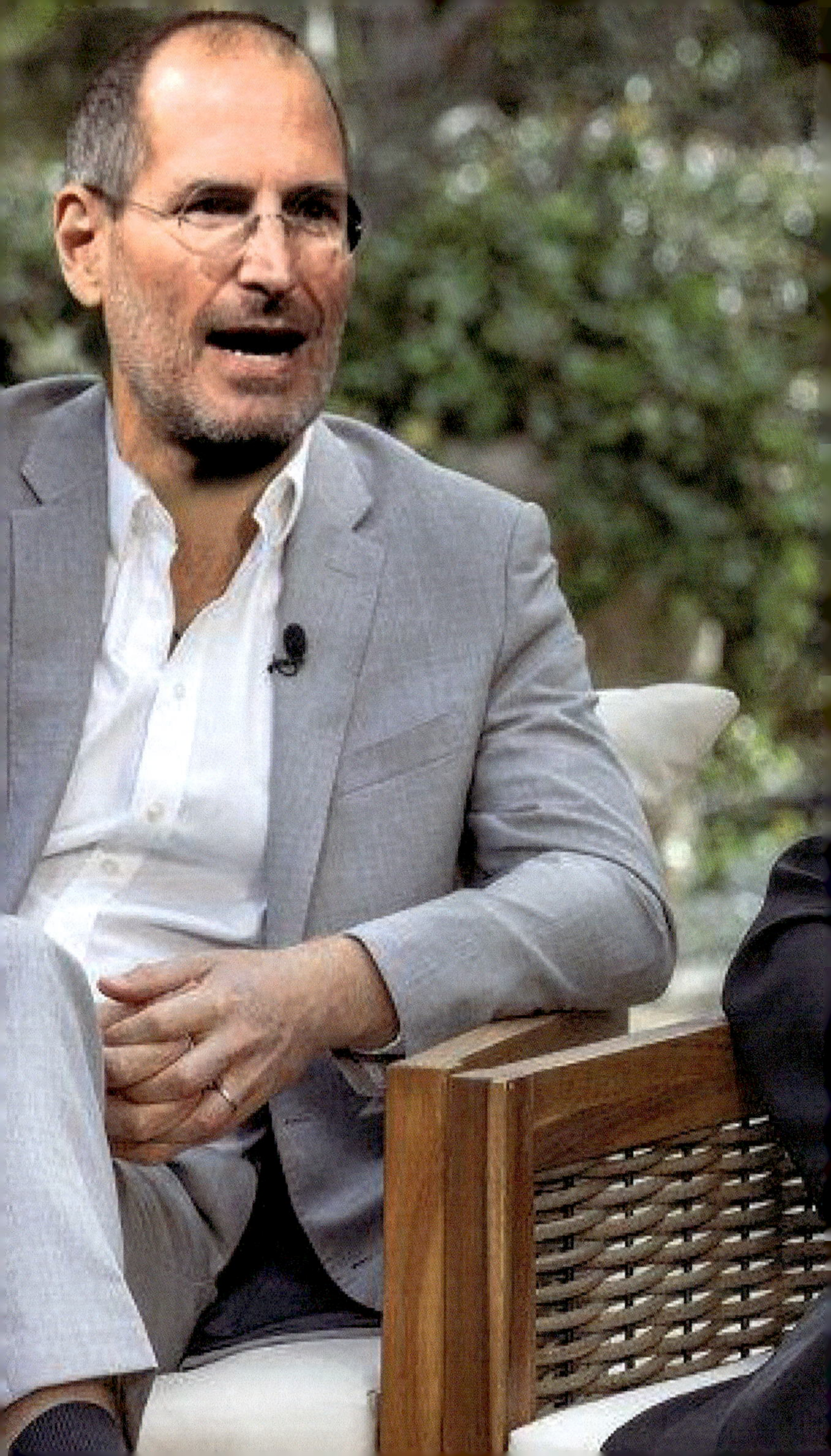

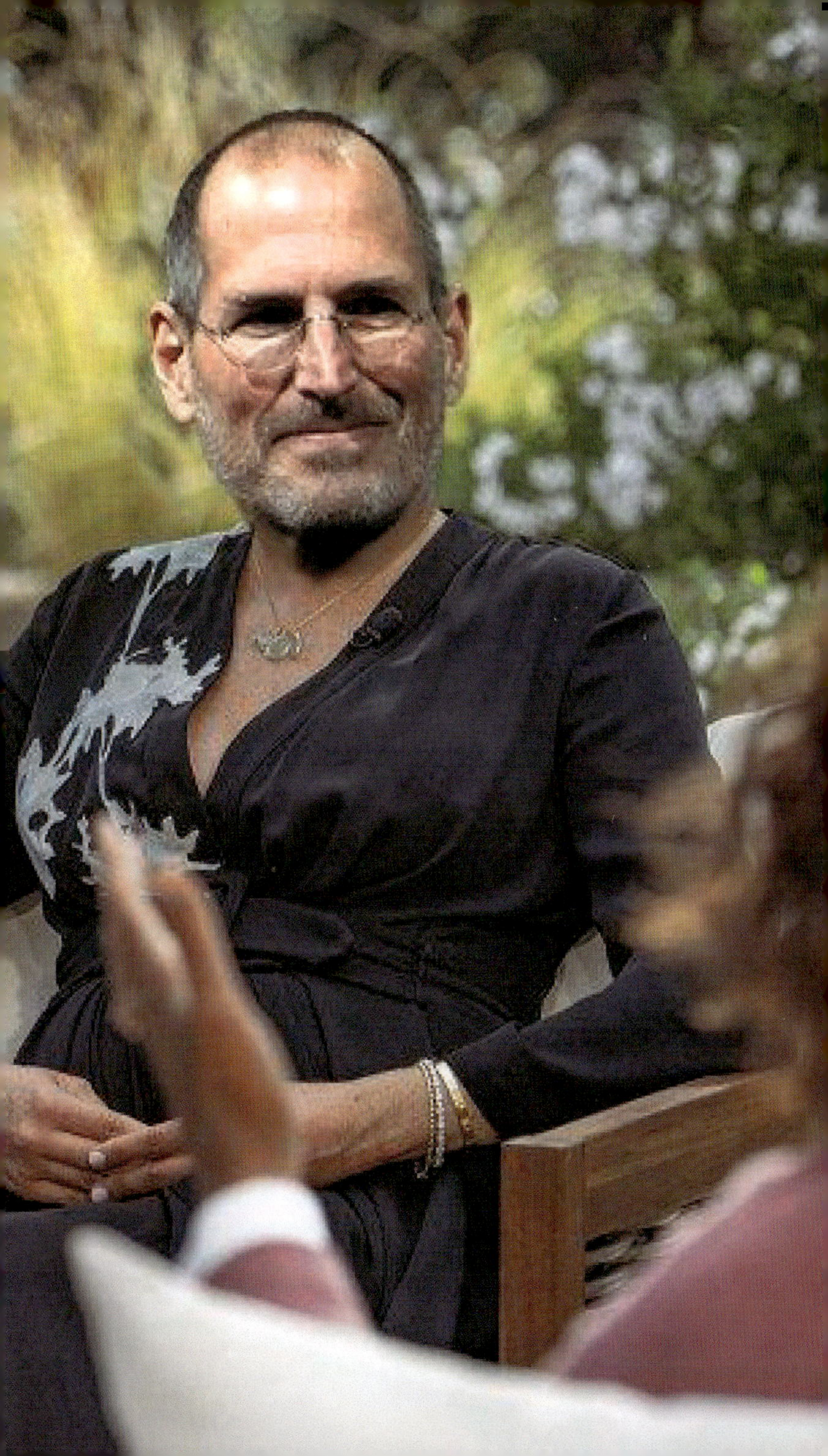

WE LOST THE RETAIL ACCOUNT YESTERDAY
OH, WHY?
BECAUSE I THOUGHT OUR LAUNCH DATE WAS A LUNCH DATE
OH, YOU!

WAS TOLD TO DEVELOP & LAUNCH BREAKTHROUGH NEW PRODUCT IN 6 MONTHS
THEN DISCOVERED PROCUREMENT NEEDS 6 MONTHS JUST TO REGISTER A NEW VENDOR

"THIS IS FINE."

When brand team is desperate for ingredient to support new claim and you work in R&D

I GOT 99 PROBLEMS...
BUT A PITCH AIN'T ONE

VEGAN

HAVING
PRE-VEGAN
FLASHBACKS

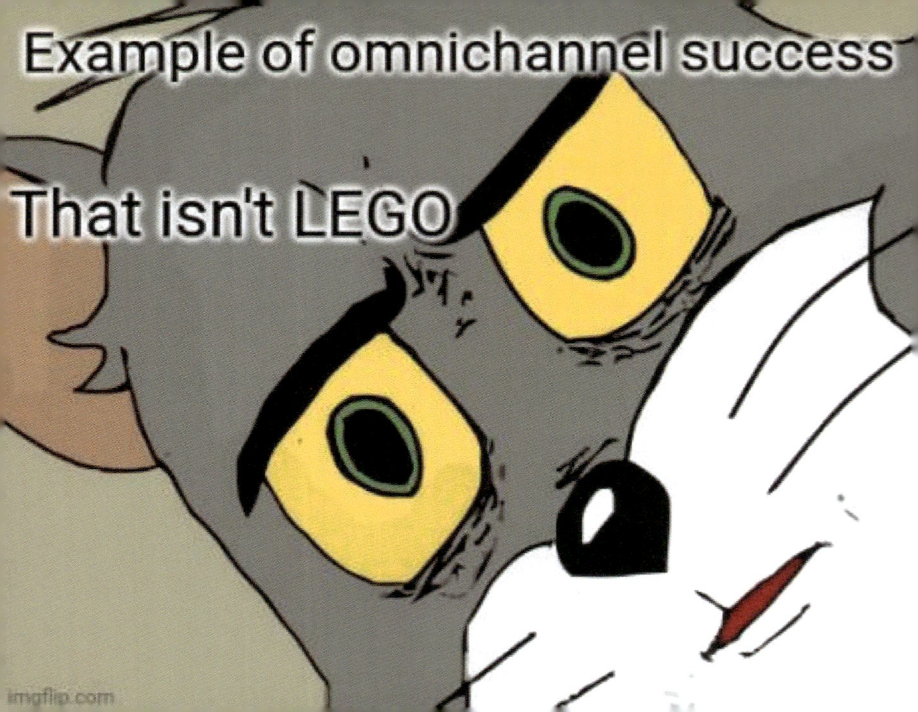
Example of omnichannel success
That isn't LEGO
imgflip.com

I GOT 99 PROBLEMS...
BUT A PITCH AIN'T ONE

We have completely lost sight of our customers' needs!
Let's commission a segmentation study!
Or NPS!
Or we could go meet some?

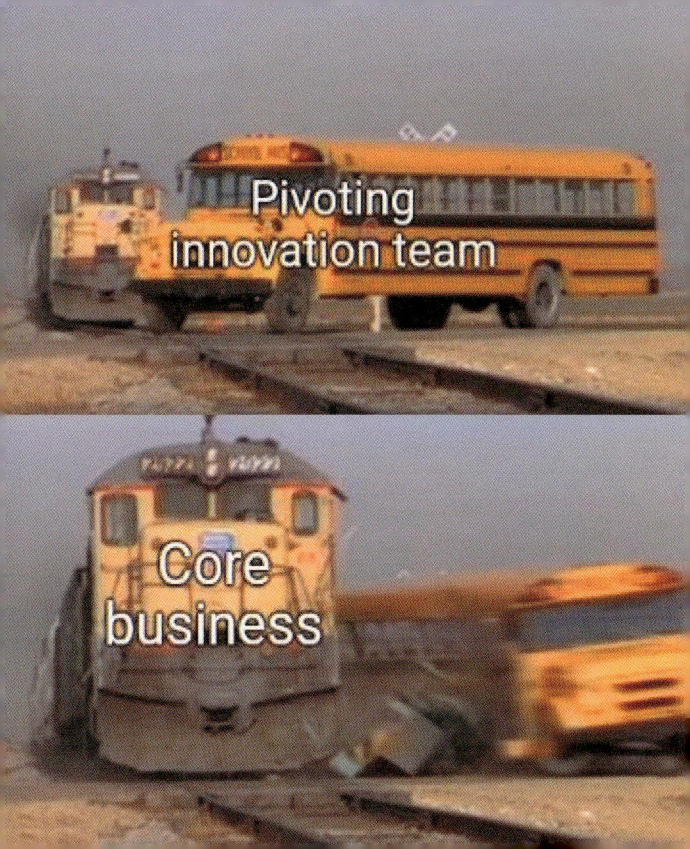
Pivoting innovation team
Core business

I CAN'T FIND ENOUGH RESPONDENTS WHO USE PRODUCT A OR B
I'LL RELAX THE CRITERIA
FIND ME THOSE WHO USE A AND B
Gudin.

I GOT 99 PROBLEMS...
BUT A PITCH AIN'T ONE

ACCELERATION, EFFICIENCY GAIN AND QUALITY YOU WANT?

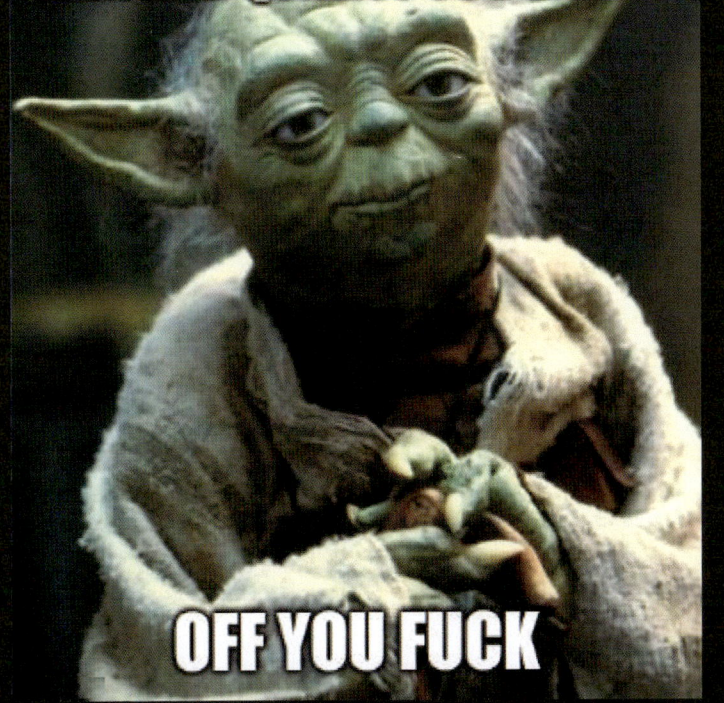

OFF YOU FUCK

Are you sure you wouldn't be better off disrupting someone else's category rather than your own?

Well yes, but actually no

I GOT 99 PROBLEMS...
BUT A PITCH AIN'T ONE

> I FEEL A LITTLE DISJOINTED
>
> NONSENSE, I DESIGNED YOU USING EXCEL SHEETS

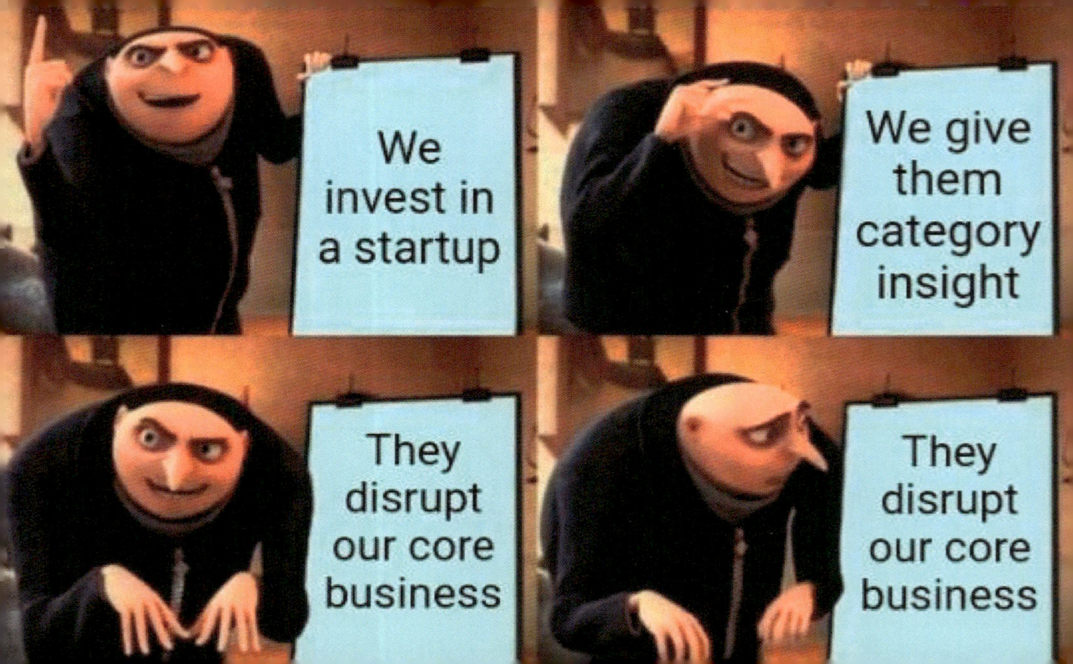

We give them category insight	They disrupt our core business
We invest in a startup	They disrupt our core business

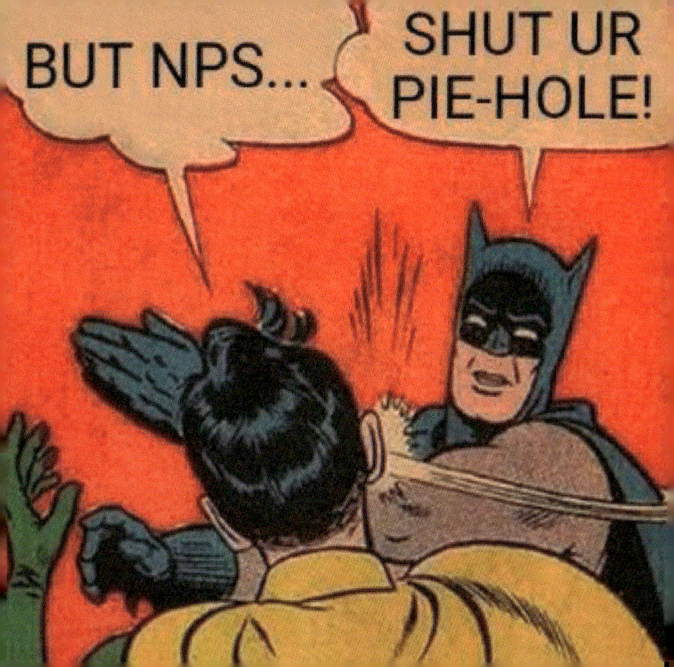
BUT NPS...
SHUT UR PIE-HOLE!

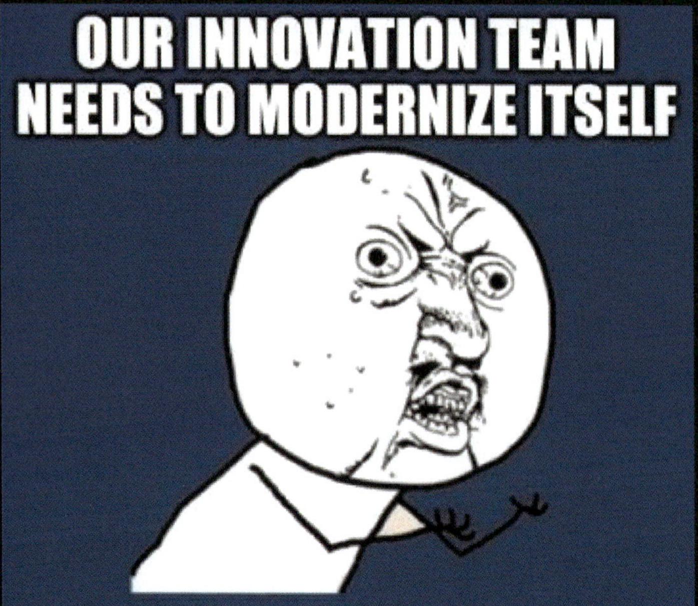
OUR INNOVATION TEAM
NEEDS TO MODERNIZE ITSELF
NO

**I GOT 99 PROBLEMS...
BUT A PITCH AIN'T ONE**

TELL ME AGAIN

HOW YOUR BRAND TRACKER SAVED THE DAY

MORE SINGLE MINDED BENEFITS

YUP, NEED MORE OF THEM.

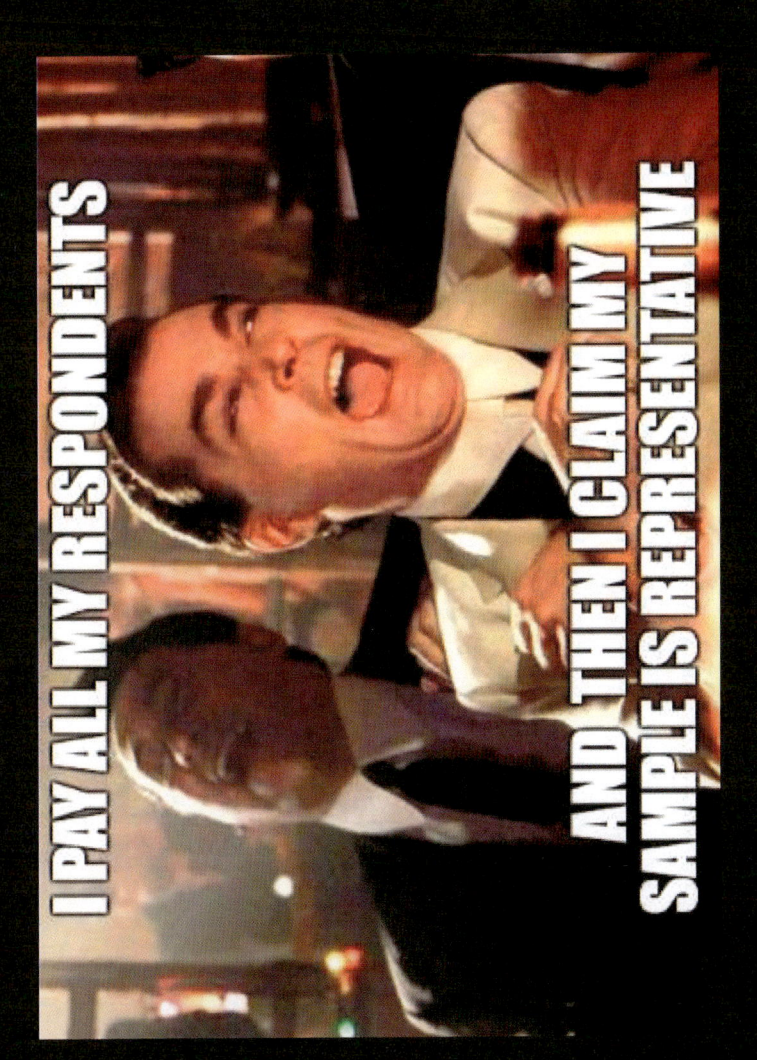

I GOT 99 PROBLEMS...
BUT A PITCH AIN'T ONE

I PAY ALL MY RESPONDENTS AND THEN I CLAIM MY SAMPLE IS REPRESENTATIVE

DID YOU HEAR THE CARTON BOX COMPANY WAS IN TROUBLE?

THEY FOLDED

WE BUILT OURSELVES

A DIGITAL ECOSYSTEM

HEY GIRL

"AMBITION" BEFORE "EXPLORATION" BEFORE "IDEA" BEFORE "PLANNING" BEFORE "SUCCESS". BUT ONLY IN THE DICTIONARY.

**I GOT 99 PROBLEMS...
BUT A PITCH AIN'T ONE**

LOOK ME IN THE EYE AND TELL ME YOU NEVER DISCOUNT

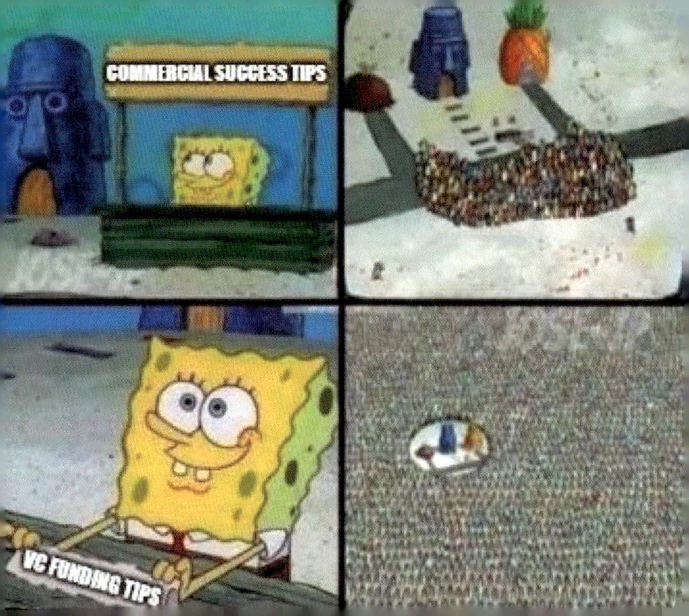
COMMERCIAL SUCCESS TIPS
VC FUNDING TIPS

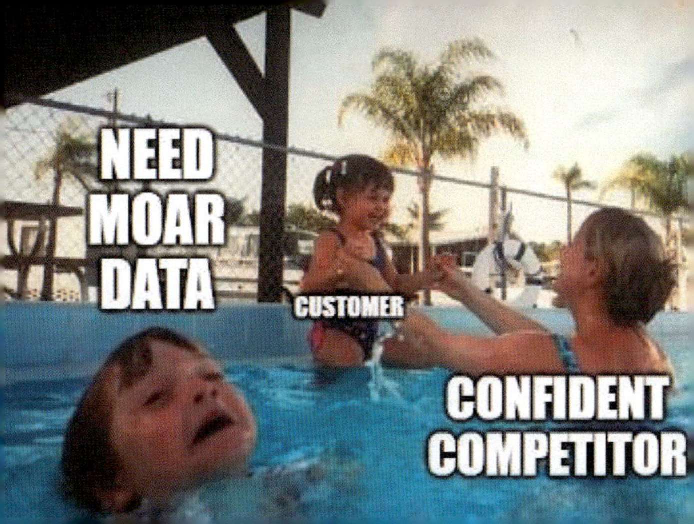
NEED
MOAR
DATA
CUSTOMER
CONFIDENT
COMPETITOR

Concepts should be written in first person!

Do you know that feeling of being wrong?

**I GOT 99 PROBLEMS...
BUT A PITCH AIN'T ONE**

HANDING OVER TO SUCESSOR

UR DEVELOPMENT PIPELINE

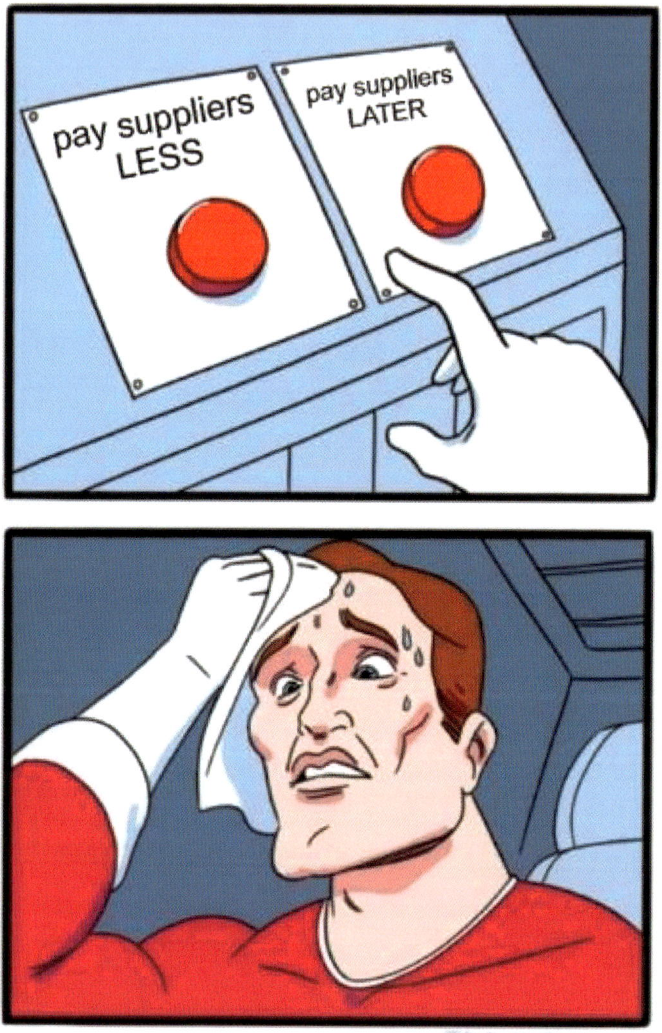

JAKE-CLARK.TUMBLR

I GOT 99 PROBLEMS...
BUT A PITCH AIN'T ONE

LOGGING SALES

WTF... ONLY TWO WKS TO Q4 CLOSURE

GET ME Q1 FORECAST FFS

PULL. DEM. FORWAAARD!!

DAWG, YO MOMMA'S SO FAT SHE MAKES N=1 QUANT RESEARCH

I GOT 99 PROBLEMS...
BUT A PITCH AIN'T ONE

ANY INSECURITY

ASK CONSUMERS

EVERY F-ING STARTUP BURNS CASH LIKE THERE'S NO TOMORROW

MY EBIT DROPS 0.1 POINTS AND THE WORLD FALLS APART

WRITING CLIENT PROPOSALS

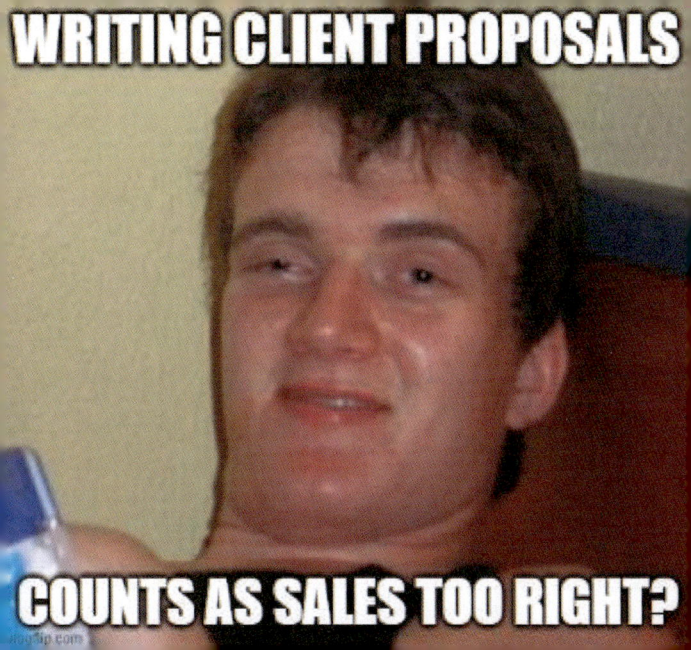

COUNTS AS SALES TOO RIGHT?

BRACE YOURSELF

ANNUAL PLANNING & PPT REFORMATTING IS COMING

I GOT 99 PROBLEMS...
BUT A PITCH AIN'T ONE

I GOT 99 PROBLEMS

BUT A PITCH AIN'T ONE

Printed in Poland
by Amazon Fulfillment
Poland Sp. z o.o., Wrocław